Cover and inside cover: "Winter Moon" by Debby Neely

I never felt compelled to collaborate with a photographer until I discovered, here in my own county, the pictures of Judy VanderMaten, which I admired from the start on an uncommon level. I began haunting shows and galleries to collect her work.

For nearly twenty years, Judy and I have been seeking a way to mount a book of our work, side by side. Most of the forty-four poems in this collection were inspired directly by Judy's images, or by the same land- and water-scapes from which she draws. Now, most happily, our friends at Columbia River Reader Press have created a book beyond what we'd ever imagined.

The poems and pictures all derive from the tidal, or estuarine, stretch of the river — what might also be called the Lower Columbia. Seek not an exact correlation between each poem and its accompanying image. We don't envision the verses as captions for the pictures nor the images as illustrations of the poems, rather as evocations of one another.

As for the "field guide" motif, these are images and words captured in hopes of furnishing for you a new kind of aesthetic, imaginative, and yes, even factual guide to our oh-so-luckily shared home: the Tidewater Reach.

~ Robert Michael Pyle

The Tidewater Reach

Field Guide
to the
Lower Columbia River
in
Poems and Pictures

Robert Michael Pyle
Judy VanderMaten

COLUMBIA RIVER READER PRESS

THE TIDEWATER REACH

Field Guide to the Lower Columbia
River in Poems and Pictures

by Robert Michael Pyle and Judy VanderMaten

PUBLISHED BY
Columbia River Reader Press
Longview, Washington
copyright MMXX
All Rights Reserved

PRINTED
in the United State of America.

The scanning, uploading and distribution of this book via the Internet or via any other means without the permission of the publisher is illegal and punishable by law. Please purchase only authorized electronic editions, and to not participate in or encourage electronic piracy of copyrighted materials.

Your support of the authors' rights is appreciated.

ISBN NUMBER: 978-1-7346725-1-0

For additional information or
to order additional copies:
Columbia River Reader Press
1333 14th Avenue
Longview, WA 98632
publisher@crreader.com

Design and Layout: Susan Piper
Editing and Captions: Hal Calbom

Cover and Inside Cover: "Winter Moon"
Woodcut by Debby Neely

Frontispiece:
"River Buoy, Mid-river Moon"
Photograph by Judy VanderMaten

River buoys aid ship navigation and are maintained by the United States Coast Guard. Solid green buoys are odd-numbered; solid red even-numbered. Buoys are moored to the river bottom and their numbers increase sequentially from the sea upriver. They denote key navigation features, not river miles.

www.crreader.com/crrpress

And this our life,
exempt from public haunt,
Finds tongues in trees,
books in the running brooks,
Sermons in stones,
and good in every thing.

~ William Shakespeare
As You Like It

CONTENTS

Bretz's Flood	13
Part One: Flood	**17**
River Cutters	19
Cottonwoods in March: Willow Grove	23
Lesser Lives	25
Boats x 3	27
A Moon I Didn't See	29
Biologia rediviva I: Enhydra lutris	31
River Pubs: River Mile 38	35
Piling Islands	37
Biologia rediviva II: Come Home Condor	43
Part Two: Neap	**45**
River Pubs: Desdemona Club	47
The Big Wave	49
I Cover the Waterfront	55
Pencil Shavings	57
Ship Report	61
Lux Sit	63
River Pubs: On Duffy's Deck	67
On the Ferry Oscar B.	69
River Pubs: Ahle's Cabin	71
The Book Boat	75
Part Three: Spring	**81**
One More Crosses the Bar	85
Gulls at Rest	87
Riverwalks	89

91	River Pubs: In the Fort George Taproom
97	Spring Comes to Altoona
99	River Monsters
103	River Pubs: At the Duck
105	Goodnight to the Gillnetters
111	New Year's Eve on Puget Island
115	When Sam McKinney Put Out from Kelley Point
119	Road to the River
121	A River and Its Mountains
123	**Part Four: Ebb**
127	Once Upon Brookfield
129	I Cross the Columbia
133	Christmas on the Columbia
135	Small Craft Advisory
137	Dredge Spoils
139	Two Rivers
143	What the Muskrat Saw
145	Ceremony
151	River Pubs: The View From Maria's
153	Fetching the Old Town at Scappoose
157	Long Dock
161	All Fall Down
163	Biographical Sketches
165	Acknowledgments
171	A Conversation with Robert Michael Pyle

Bretz's Flood

It starts in the furnace of the core,
rises through the mantle's crush.
Makes the crust, then breaks on through
in plutons, vents, volcanoes. Dike swarms leak
across the land like Vaseline on hot skin.
Congeal in lava flows called Roza,
Elephant Gap and Rattlesnake Ridge,
Umatilla, Pomona, and Selah. Flow,
then freeze in lichen-daubed
entablature and colonnade,
all the way to the sea.

After Pangaea, continents surfed
the crusted waves, broke their backs
against far shores, forging the shapes we know.
Plates of the shelf shoulder plates
of the land, bunch them up in the middle,
raise the Rockies from nothing more
than force and dust. Where mountains crumple
upward, before crumbling down again, a moment
comes when, high enough, they tempt
the snows that crown the years. Then press,
and press, and press some more,
till glaciers start to move.

As cold goes south, the ice sheets grow,
till half the continent goes under.
Polish, scour, lathe, and grind — leave
sign of ice on granite domes, the scream
of ice on unforgetting stone. Rivers drain
the glaciers, but Clark Fork is plugged:

two thousand feet of ancient ice,
two hundred miles of inland sea.
Then warming, and melting,
time after time for a thousand years,
till the dam breaks through!
Then Glacial Lake Missoula is loosed
upon the land. Down pours deluge,
downhill, down-grade, down-map —
ten times the flow of all the rivers of the world.

Cut the coulees, channel scablands,
carve basalt like old black butter; even gouge
that great green slot that we will call the Gorge.

Slash Grand Coulee! Swamp Dry Falls!
Shoot Wallula Gap, whack Beacon Rock,
shatter the very Bridge of the Gods,
before they're even named. Never
so much water, sluicing to the sea,
with such a force of will — sloshing
from wall to black rock wall, from
rimrock to rimrock, four hundred feet deep —
until, the ice all gone,
the river finds its level,
never looking back
at the havoc
it's left behind —

where all
that remains
is geology.

Part One

Flood

The gravitational force of the Moon and the Sun pulls at the Earth's water and creates the tides. The change from low tide to high tide is known as a *flood tide*. The difference in depth between high and low tides during any particular cycle is the *tidal range*. Where rivers and ocean tides meet, the extent to which the saltwater reaches upstream and mingles with the river's fresh water is the *Tidewater Reach*.

River Cutters

Hollowed cottonwoods, burnt, scraped, adzed,
maybe the first craft to ply the river's face.
Canoes, by the time of the beaver hunters,
voyageurs with bottomless skill, paddled
all across the continent, headwater to headwater
and down again, all the way to Vancouver.

Long time later, it's all kayaks, cottonwood
and birch gone to plastic and fiberglass.
They look like so many gummi worms
lined up along the dock, belly down. Then
put in, and turn into fish, slicing
the whitecaps of the main stem, cutting
whitewater in the steep rocky tribs.

Hunting thrills instead of pelts,
oneness with water mediated
by thin skins of red, yellow, blue, watching
wildlife instead of trapping. Oh, it is
a different world out there on the river,
this latter-day cutting, these Road Scholar voyageurs,
when nobody's life is on the line
and only the cormorants take a second look.

KAYAKS: SKAMOKAWA DOCK

Sea kayakers flourish on the Columbia. At Skamokowa the interplay of tides and river flow creates exhilarating — and potentially hazardous — shifts in current. Inshore sloughs and inlets offer calmer water, bird watching and pristine vistas.

Cottonwoods in March: Willow Grove

After the dance, you drove out Willow Grove,
across the bridge beyond the town,
between river and backwater slough.
The warm night beguiled by cottonwoods
all along the bank, just breaking bud,
just putting out their soft green tongues,
all sticky with the brown paste of balsam,
once called Balm of Gilead. Both of you
taken by the cloying scent
far beyond sense. You knew you shouldn't park,
but you did. And stroked
each other's faces
with the soft green spears
(cheeks, eyelids, right below the greedy nostrils,
lips), lacerating your hearts beyond repair.
A pleasure so intense (the two senses least used,
smell and touch) that you could never, ever,
speak it as it was.
Barely even kissed. But you both knew —
didn't you? — that the kisses would come,
and you could only hope
they would match the sweetness
of those cottonwood strokes
on Willow Grove
that night.

Lesser Lives

Mostly, we tend to think of the big lives on the river —
the ospreys and eagles, salmon and sturgeon,
seals and sea lions and otters, and all of their ilk.
But underlying, undergirding, underwriting all those grandees
are the lesser lives, at least in matters of size.
The fry and the copepods, the worms and the gastropods,
all the large legions of invertebrates, whose mass
far exceeds that of all the migratory whales.

The surprise is how many of these little creatures
are no more native in these waters than the Chinese
cannery workers, Finnish loggers, or the name "Columbia"
itself. Whether riding Japanese tsunami or some flag's ballast,
they hail from elsewhere, just as most of us surely do.

Have you seen the yellow mayflies, big as grasshoppers
and sometimes as thick as locusts? Noted the serried drifts
of shiny olive clamshells on some wake-whacked beach?
Who knows whose bilge they came in on. But someone eats
them all, in this great flowing chowder, this soup-bowl of a river,
where we are the least life of all
in the long run.

Boats x 3

The ferry treads water in the black river,
waiting for three craft to pass: a dark barge
behind a tug, a fast freighter, another tug
pushing nothing I could see. Once they'd passed,
the engine thrummed again, beat back the current,
and we bounced across that triplet wake.

I wondered why the freighter didn't swamp
that blacknight barge, shoving it under like
a fat man on a float. I suppose the radios
keep things aright, just as my ferryman shut
his engines down in time. Vessels in midstream
always have the right-of-way.

Or does nocturnal traffic go in packs,
proof against the dark danger of the night?
Next day, in Skamokawa, along the banks
of Steamboat Slough, bright light of afternoon,
their plot came clear.

Three gillnetters lay at anchor beneath
a rusting boatshed, full and upswept hulls
facing into the dropping tide, side by side, and ready.
So, when night falls into the slough,
they'll break their lines and join the others,
out there plying the river's murk together.

A Moon I Didn't See

Was it low and red,
that moon you saw
above the river mouth?
The color of a dull ache
long after a fall,
when it rose?

I didn't see it, so I don't know;
but I've seen moons that ached like that before.

Last night
another moon cruised
the ceiling of the fog, glanced
off the tin-roofed bridge
like a discus
thrown the old way,
skidding to a stop
in the river's moonglade.

I'd like to think of every moon
as mine
despite my absent eyes. Maybe
it's the moons you never see
that burn the deepest.

Biologia rediviva I: Enhydra lutris

When Robert Gray in *Columbia Rediviva*
crossed the bar and entered the mouth in 1792,
he carried copper trinkets and nails, sent
by his employers, the Mssrs. Bullfinch of Boston,
in expectation of silk, spices, and other Asian riches
in return: an alchemy wrought through the medium
of the rich, deep pelage of sea otters.

Between the Russians and the rest,
over the following years, the Steller's
sea cows, the auks, and the sea otters
went all to hell. Long gone, long gone,
from these waters. But wait! There's more.

Brought from Amchitka to LaPush in 1969,
sea otters have spread again along the coast.
Forty years later, more than 200 years
since Robert Gray came for them,
the first *Enhydra lutris* showed up again
at the mouth of the Columbia.

It's not easy. The water is warmer,
more acid, full of plastic, and rising.
It'll take the kelp beds, the sea urchins,
and all the rest, to really bring them back.

But who knows? Maybe the name itself
    — *Columbia Rediviva* —
(first American ship to circle the earth)
will take on a new sense. So that when we think
of this river, instead of Columbus, we may think
of the *Rediviva* part:

a river, an otter, revived.

PILINGS PATH: ASTORIA

Few rivers are so influenced by tides and weather. The very height of river pilings, and the docks and ramps that either float up and down with them or are permanently affixed to them, anticipates tidal fluctuations well over ten feet. Among the most unanticipated, and aggravating, hazards of Lewis and Clark's visit to the Lower Columbia was the tidal movement, which disrupted their camps and their forward progress.

River Pubs: River Mile 38

The best time to go is in the snow,
which is even more uncommon
than the opening hours of this place.
Never mind if it's closed — sure, the beer's
grand, but the location is even better.
Go down, past the marina, the cabins,
the yurts. Sit on the gelid ground
beside the shore, where cottonwoods
revel in their rare adornment. Watch
ducks and geese on the water, dappled
by the downy fall of snowflakes. Imagine
summer on the back deck of the pub,
since the grass is always greener,
or on some sailboat at rest by the dock,
and ask, was ever a watering hole
better blessed by placement? Beside
Grand Union Canal, Lago Lugano
or Lake Windermere, little creek
in Enterprise, Oregon? Surely not.
And there's Maria's taco stand to boot!
Well, it's even better in the winter,
when you are the only patron,
besides the black cottonwoods,
in the snow. Life is rich!
And so it goes.

Piling Islands

Long after the old canneries have gone down,
the ferry docks turned to kindling,
the net-sheds sunk among glittering scales
and rotting nets in the funky sediments below,
rows and rows of old wood pilings survive.
Whole forests of Doug-fir that today would fill
whole convoys of log trucks — better logs
than all the standing stumpage in the doghair,
in these days of peckerwood poles.

Each piling an island. A 3-D patch of habitat poking
out of the aqueous humor of the river's eye.
Many have small forests on their tops. My favorites,
in the backwater docks — spinneys of pilings on
the Gray's, the John Day, the Clatskanine, Elokomin,
where plant life proliferates the more and a single pile
may be crowned with a Rod Stewart mop of twenty
species: grass and sedge, rush and yarrow, trefoil and
jewelweed, two kinds of asters and even white orchids,
all the insects you might imagine attendant upon them.
Removing these pilings would be a clearcut all over
again, of dire consequence to legions of life.

Canoeing the Gray's down to its self-named bay,
beside the spruce swamp, takes me past Devil's Elbow.
There in the crook wobble six or eight old pilings,
each topped by a hemlock. Was I the only one,
I wondered, who noticed the perfect bonsai
crowning one of the piles? Then one day

my friend Diane saw me adrift among the gray
stand, even as Moses in his rushes. Later she asked:
"Have you seen Kyle's bonsai?" Her canny son
had clipped it thus, these several years. That's when
I knew I wasn't the only one in love
with these river-sticks and their crowns.
Long may they last!

COLUMBIA LIGHTSHIP: ASTORIA

The US Coast Guard Lightship *Columbia* is one of six surviving "floating lighthouses" used in especially hazardous waterways. *Columbia* was commissioned in 1951 and crewed by 18. She left service in 1979, replaced by a remote-controlled buoy. Tours of the lightship are included with admission to the Columbia River Maritime Museum.

LOWER COLUMBIA: CANNERIES

Between 1866 and 1870, 35 canneries on the Lower Columbia packed more than 60,000 cases of salmon yearly, 48 pounds per case. Difficult and labor-intensive businesses, canneries were plagued with contentious issues, including use of immigrant workers and struggles over wages and union representation.

Biologia rediviva II: Come Home Condor

The Corps of Discovery found
California condors at the Columbia's
teeming mouth in 1805 and 1806.
This seems astonishing in our time,
when the last few wild condors
were taken in, to try to save them.

Over the next few years
they were captive bred,
and on a wing and a prayer,
put back out in southwest places
like the Vermilion Cliffs
and the Ventana Wilderness.
Where, happily, they took.

So that now I have to ask:
if sea otters may come back
to the Columbia, could
condors be far behind?
Like ospreys and eagles
after *Silent Spring*,
will even these once more soar
above long-lonesome shores?

Part Two

Neap

Tides are products of gravitational interaction among the Earth, the Sun, and the Moon. Because the Moon is so much closer, it exerts a greater effect on the tides. *Tidal range* is the result of juxtapositions of the three bodies. When they align, and the Moon is either a new moon or a full moon, the tidal range is most extreme. On the other hand, tidal range is least during the two "half" moons each month, when the orbs are out of alignment, and counteract each other. The result is a Neap Tide, from the Anglo-Saxon, meaning *without the power.*

River Pubs: Desdemona Club ~ A Gray Day on Gray's Bay

Or it would be, if you could see it. There's no river
view from the Dirty D, in spite of its famous portholes.
There's also no well Scotch for Happy Hour. Only bourbon,
American whiskey. The only Scotch at all is Johnny Black,
at six-fifty per. This, in a town founded by Scots!
But the shuffleboard in the back is free, Nirvana's on the air,
and I am almost alone on a Monday afternoon in March.
One or two at the bar to keep the pink-haired barmaid company,
a couple more clinging to the video poker.

But if you could see out, and through the shot-streaming rain,
and if you happened to look north, across the river,
it would be a very gray day on Gray's Bay. Put out
into that murk, turn left like a bar pilot, and with luck
you'll come to the bridge. Beyond lie the Desdemona Sands
where as many ill-starred seamen have come to grief
as have belly-up to the bar in the Dirty D, this dive also named
for the unlucky chick in *Othello*, here at the dark end of town.

Just think: had it been a gray day on Gray's Bay on May 11, 1792,
when Robert Gray crossed the Bar in the *Columbia Rediviva*,
there would be no Gray's Bay. The Columbia might be named
Vancouver's River. And the well whiskey at the Dirty D?
It would be Canadian.

The Big Wave

(after Robinson Jeffers, "November Surf")

When the autumn tides arrive each year,
big waves come ashore and wash the beach
like a giant sponge. Come winter, the storms hit
harder yet, and scrape the shoreline clean.

When the big wave comes
When the big wave comes

The valleys beyond and the hills above
are jealous of that seaside purging. They abide,
and imagine such a bath as would scour
the cumbered continent free of its dirty old blot.

When the big wave comes
When the big wave comes

But when the plates finally slip, as plates will do,
and the big wave comes ashore,
all insults will be washed away
and the land again come clean.

When the big wave comes
When the big old mama wave comes
When the big wave comes on down,

And after that wave, as Robinson Jeffers wrote,
the humans will be fewer, the hawks more common,
the rivers pure from mouth to source —
and we'll know again at last what it's like to live
on a coast made fresh once more.

When the Big Wave Comes
When the Big Wave Comes
When the Big...Wave... .

RIVER VILLAGE: CATHLAMET

Cathlamet remains the only incorporated town in Wahkiakum, the smallest of Washington's counties, and is the site of one of the region's oldest Native American villages. The name "Cathlamet" (Kathlamet) is said to come from the local Chinookan language referring to the area as a "rocky shore." Cathlamet became the Wahkiakum County seat in 1854 and was officially incorporated in 1907. The old waterfront still hosts tugboat operations, boat building, and other commercial businesses.

I Cover the Waterfront

(Ilwaco, December, 2018: For Karla)

Sometimes it seems the hopes of all mankind lie
on display in a small-town bookstore, against
all odds still open on a bleak December dock
in a time when so much else is going, going, gone.

After the reading I spill out the back door
onto the wet green waterfront. Walk
up and down in the dripping dusk. The slips
still have boats, though the fleet is tiny now.

Still, a good seafood grill, a pub, and Jessie's
Fish Market at the end of the pier, persist.
I remember charters by the dozen, the cafe
at the end of the spit, Doupe's Hardware

as a going concern. But now it's mostly a matter
of the riverfront, where the Columbia brushes
Baker Bay before dying, or being born anew,
into the Ocean itself. And what moves me

is not what's gone, but what somehow remains:
the boats, the oysters, the books shiny in the light
through the wet window. They speak to the possibility
of all things, even in these times, waterfronts do.

As long as little seaside towns live on, giving harbor
to half-forgotten craft and vagabonds on a winter's night,
I will continue to cover the waterfront, seeking something
not likely to be found, anywhere else.

Pencil Shavings

I love the brown butterflies that fly
among canyon walls, where the scent is juniper,
that flit above San Luis Valley's floor
— Nabokov's satyrs, Alamosa wood nymphs —
flecks of fawn and otter on the wing. How
their papery vanes make hope
from nothing but nectar and dust.

Yesterday in Astoria, a world away
from San Luis, I moved my desk. Discovered
in a disused drawer a small paper bag:
pencil shavings I'd somehow kept. How
could I throw them in the trash now,
having saved them all this time?
The open window winked.
Without a thought, I cast
the cedar chips out the window.
onto the crabshell breeze.

Pale brown butterflies flickered past the wall,
all down to the valley pavement of the street —
and for a moment, the scent was juniper.

HIGHS AND LOWS

Due to the river's extreme tidal range, the canneries used pilings elevated well above the surface to accommodate tidal fluctuations. Most of today's piling remnants are short, rotted and continuing to erode. The few high pilings remaining evoke the elevated life among the canneries, the network of ladders and ramps that accommodated the shifting tides, and the fishermen and work gangs laboring 24 hours a day during rich salmon runs.

Ship Report

Nine ships on the river today
four outside, five inside Tongue Point,
how I count them. Each morning
the radio station gives the Ship Report, telling
who's here, where from and where to,
and what they carry, potash, grain, logs, cars.
Most of them have black tops, white bridges.
and red hulls, but sometimes blue, or green.

Since 9/11 and the Patriot Act, the happy sight
of crewmen traipsing the town is behind us. No more
parties for Russian sailors, no Asian men
in watch caps and pea coats schlepping bags:
gifts and goods bound for Seoul, or Manila.
Now the greeting committee and only customs official:
this great blue heron hunched on rotten piling, exacting
duty from anyone who thinks of coming ashore —
tribute paid solely in the coin of cold raindrops,
falling on his sodden plume.

Lux Sit

From the blue table at Mo's she watches
the pilot boat lights creep into the docks.
Yellow lights on the bridge span glimmer,
red ones flash, reflect off the river below.
Travelers' lights flicker past the guardrails.
Green navigational lights show where to go,
where not. Lights on the ships at anchor
seem unbearably sad, while lights up in town
speak of ways to spend an evening, a life,
in restaurants, night spots, theaters,
before the blue hearth of the television.

She sits at the blue table at Mo's, thinking
of all the lights, all the lives, all the ways
she might have followed this fickle river.
And how regret could equal happenstance
minus foresight, and remorse could just be content
filtered through oinks and rude breath of sea lions.

She doesn't care. There is a blue glass dolphin
on a bouncy spring stuck in a sparkly chunk of coral
on the windowsill, and a blue glass crab with a sticker
that says "I glow," both of them for sale. And there is
the glossy blue table. And there is the river,
which might be blue in certain lights. And
there is the night ahead.

She takes a sip from the blue plastic water glass
that says "Mo's" on the side, pays her bill, steps out
into the many lights of the Columbian night. Keeps
an eye out for the green ones, the navigational aids,
with no clear idea at all of what comes next.

NETS AND FLOATS

Commercial and sports fisheries on the Columbia River have been in decline since the late 1800s. Canneries established in the 1860s rapidly depleted the supply of fish, and in the early 1900s laws were passed to try to preserve the fishery. The Columbia River dams, beginning with Bonneville Dam in 1938, hastened the decline of anadromous fish, such as salmon — which are spawned in fresh water, live their lives in saltwater, then return to fresh water to spawn and die.

TOPKNOTS

River pilings in particular tidal ranges sport colorful vegetative topknots, often including several different plant varieties. Thanks to variations in fresh water levels, pilings can enjoy two nutritious "waterings" a day, of varying duration, and benefit from perpetual re-seeding from the downstream current. Canoeists even name their favorites, and follow their coiffure's development from season to season.

River Pubs: On Duffy's Deck

Only crows to be heard. Merganser
duckling, long bill ring-tipped,
pale neck and belly down, strange
to be all by itself, out there paddling
in the milky way of knotweed petals,
nebulae of cottonwood leaves,
riding the uptide flow.

Yellow-striped jumping spider leaps to my knee.
Steller's jay vaults the river, which loops
around the gravel bar under alders and elms,
ninebark and knotweed, then slingshots
down to the bay, on this 90-degree afternoon.
Wait till winter! When the river roars through here,
almost up to the deck, and I take my pint inside,
into dim orange light and endless Irish tapes.

But for now,
out here on Duffy's deck, with the crows,
the mergs, the jays, as the day drops
through 80, to 70, and less,
perfection seems possible.

Yet still my pint runs out.

On the Ferry Oscar B.
April 12, Westport to Puget Island

It's forty years ago come August I first rode this ferry.
Or this crossing, anyway — back then, even smaller,
it was the *Wahkiakum*. She charted the rest of my life's course
that day, she did, coming into this county that gave her name.

Now, in the second cold wet late April in a row,
thanks to La Niña, the sweet pang of balsam slaps
out from the yellow-green cottonwoods all along
the islands. The old bald eagle sits tousled atop a dead one.
Redheads and scaups off the bow, a few swells,
and we're already there.

River Pubs: Ahle's Cabin
(There Will Be Grebes)

Tiny log-built inn, perched
between railroad and river in Kalama.
Grateful Dead mellow on Pandora
black cabernet, yellow lights, no one
loud as they bend their elbows, trading
stories of the Amalfi Coast: "We caught
the ferry to Capri." "Oh, we did that too,"
Almost have the place to myself,
as it never will be in summer.

But now, cottonwoods finally bare,
it won't be long until they push
browny-green buds out their tips.
Already, eleven days into the year,
hazel catkins dangle and hazen
the bank bright yellow: first flower
of spring. Swarmflies glitter and dance
off the deck. "I know you rider, gonna miss me
when I'm gone" croon the Dead; "We can share
the women, we can share the wine...."

When the wine's all gone, it's back
along the beach, late January sun.
Once, the butterfly fleet fluttered here.
Now, only a minor tug, barge of unknown
burden, makes a little wake. Nothing else
disturbs the river, except every flash
and ripple ever made, and you just know,
that if you look long enough,
there will be grebes.

SLOUGH, NOT SLUFF

The local word is slough, pronounced "slew," and characterized by a variety of definitions. On the Columbia River, a slough is a backwater or inside passage of calmer water distinct from the main channel. Sloughs have had great commercial utility on the Columbia, storing log rafts, protecting boats and floating homes from the stronger current, nurturing wildlife. The identically spelled "slough," pronounced "sluff," is to cast off or discard.

MORE SHIPS, FEWER FISH

The fearsome Columbia Bar still makes ship navigation challenging, but engineers and commercial interests work relentlessly to keep the Columbia friendly to shipping. Steamboats began plying the river in the 1840s and 1850s. In 1886 jetties were built to ease currents over the bar, but risks remained, and in 1891 engineers began dredging the Columbia to create navigable ship channels upriver. Today ocean freighters can travel as far upstream as Portland and Vancouver, and barges to Lewiston, Idaho, thanks to a system of channels and locks completed in 1975.

The Book Boat

He bought a good old tub named *Lorraine*
off an old salt gone to shore on Sauvie Island.
Barely knew navigation, let alone diesel,
so come spring and still afloat, he found a mate —
a worse-off soak, never dried out, in a tavern
off lower Burnside on Water Street —
to caulk decks, pump bilge, romance
the fickle engine into life.

When it began to look like *Lorraine* might not sink,
he built shelves in the hold, and started buying
books wherever he could: Good Wills and thrifts
in The Dalles and St. Helens, library sales in Rainier
and White Salmon, the remainder tables at Powell's.
Then, recalling bookmobiles from his boyhood
on the plains, he hung his shingle on the bridge,
and took The Book Boat on the road — on the river.

And so it went, up and down the tidal reach,
Bonneville to Baker Bay and back again.
Sometimes through the locks, all the way
to Lewiston. Laying his wares before the boaters,
the fishers, the workers, the loafers, all of them
hungry for good books, though they might not know it.
He sold them cheap, gave them away, or —
his favorite — bartered, for fish, fruit, or laundry.
Swapped a late Brian Doyle for a sturgeon,
Middlemarch for Maryhill wine. Made enough
for ground beef, beer, and diesel. Even the cat got fed
and the mate paid enough for drunken leave ashore.

Lorraine became a legend, up and down the river.
Marinas vied for her, gave free moorage for a night
or three. Until he started to wonder about the islands,
the Inside Passage, and beyond. So he took *Lorraine*
across the bar, and didn't die. Put in at LaPush,
where he sold all of his Pushkin to a Russian emigré,
and a set of Twilight to a wannabe werewolf. Then east
up the Straits: Neah Bay, Sekiu, P.A., P.T.,
and Points North. Last rumors came from Kodiak.
But even now the Columbia remembers. And there's
always a slip open, just in case.

HISTORY

Native American peoples inhabited the Lower Columbia for thousands of years. The first Europeans to sight the river's mouth were probably Spanish explorers around 1775. The Boston trader Robert Gray sailed up the Columbia in 1792 and named the river for his ship. The Lewis and Clark Expedition wintered at its mouth in 1805-1806 and an English geographer, David Thompson, later explored most of the river for the North West Company.

Part Three

Spring

The difference between high and low tide is greatest at the new moon and full moon. During these phases the solar tide and lunar tide coincide, because the sun and moon are both aligned with Earth, magnifying the gravitational force. This alignment is known as *syzygy*. The resulting tides are called king tides or *spring* tides. The name has nothing to do with the season of the year; it's a synonym for "jump" or "leap." If a spring tide coincides with either the spring or autumnal equinox, expect the largest tidal range of the year: At the equinoxes both moon and sun are also aligned with the equator.

POWERFUL PILINGS

Among the strongest of foundations, river pilings have remarkable durability, despite their common appearance of decrepitude. Like so much on the river, most piling remnants on the Lower Columbia are created by the tidal extremes. Pilings that remain underwater are remarkably durable and decay-resistant. The wooden pilings underpinning the city of Venice, for instance, are estimated to be more than a thousand years old. It's the combination of water and oxygen — repeated exposure to air at low tides — that rots the tops off the pilings.

FERRY FOG

The last ferry operating on the Lower Columbia is the *Oscar B*, which replaced its long-time predecessor, the *Wahkiakum*. From the Washington side, ferry riders leave Cathlamet and cross a bridge to Puget Island, where they board the ferry for the 15-minute crossing. *Oscar B* holds 19 vehicles and is owned and operated by Wahkiakum County. It drops passengers hourly at the Oregon-side town of Westport, just downriver from Clatskanie.

One More Crosses the Bar
(Carlton Appelo, May 12, 1922 – February 12, 2019)

Born on a fishing boat out of Deep River,
on the way to the hospital in Astoria.
Did a thousand things over 96 years.
Studied in Sweden, captained
a Black infantry unit in the war, ran
our independent telephone company
nigh on forever. Published histories
of the river towns in his phone books —
he knew a captive audience! Married
Berenice, and loved her all those years.

"Yes, we will gather at the river, the beautiful
the beautiful river." At the Valley Bible we sing
the hymns, honor this lefty Swedish Finn
of a puckish Christian peacemaker, remember
his corny, off-color jokes at Grange: "What's
the difference between a Norwegian and a Swede?"
he'd ask, then answer: "The Norwegians invented
the toilet seat, but the Swedes put the hole in it."

Didn't die on a boat on the river, as he was born.
But "from out our bourne of Time and Place"
an indispensable man was well sent off today, even
as Arthur to Avalon, when Carlton crossed the bar.
Just, I'd say, what Tennyson had in mind,
though to his loss, he never saw this particular bar.

Gulls at Rest

On the bridge lie gray lumps like so many
dust-bunnies blowing in the wakes of trucks,
plucked and pummeled by the river wind.
From the Astoria Bridge you see wraiths
rising in the morning sun from sandbar humps:
divots from the dredge's work, haunted by fogs
and damps escaping river mud, too light to stay
behind.

Every drain-hole clogged with grass, like so many
green muffs. How the wind howls through,
how the spindrift catches in those stranded
turves. All above the rails the gulls float past,
sickle-wristed, playing with the wind, eyeing
the sands for stranded clams and fish. Lighter
than the river-wraiths, too light to fall
below.

It's the young gray gulls that go down,
missing the practiced flick of wing that tips
a weightless body away from death. Gray
tumps of feather and bone that blow
away in time, fertilize the drain-hole grass, settle
into mizzling rain and rising wraiths, but never blend
with bridge. Too heavy to live, too light to fly
anymore.

Riverwalks

are the same everywhere, except how they're not.
One shoreline promenade is a lot like another, tugging
the body along the waterline, a chance to move
the muscles, to dampen the mind and its muddles
in the generous lap of wake, and wind, and wonder.

And there is company, if desired. Is it white
pelicans and egrets with plumes like
high cirrus clouds in high winds
on a Mexican lakeside malecon? Or magpies
and kingfishers of a mid-continent canyon?
Or the sea lions and sea otters and herons haunting
Monterey docks or northern riversides
near their sea-dumps? Rafts of western grebes?
Cottonwoods or palms, willows, alders, or mimosas?

And always and everywhere, dogs...lots of dogs.

For towns that haven't yet sacrificed their shorelines
to industry, rip-rap, or roadways
(or have grabbed them back again),
there is something about a riverwalk
they will never regret, for which the citizens
will always thank them.

Call it a grace note on existence.
Call it wet. Call it a chance to step back
and consider where to stand now,
at the moist edge,
where we once stepped out.

River Pubs: In the Fort George Taproom

So what did they expect?
Mr. Astor wanted to corner all the furs
of the Far Northwest — last of the unclaimed peltries.
So he sent both a ship and a party by land,
in the near wake of Lewis and Clark.
But lacking Jefferson's hiring skills, Astor chose
a strict Navy man to command an unruly crew
of French-Canadian voyageurs,
each his own man, around the Horn.
They nearly mutineed the first night out!
And when the *Tonquin* finally made the mouth
of the Great River of the West? Fed up
with them all, Captain Thorn ordered boat
after ship's boat across the stormy bar,
and of course they died.

After offloading most of the others
on the Oregon side, Thorn scooted north
into hostile waters, eager to trade for pelts,
but absent any manners, or respect. When he kicked
their furs in their faces, the Indians took out
their knives. The sole surviving white hid in the hold
and blew up the powder magazines, killing
all aboard. And who would have wondered?

Astor's expedition by land fared almost as badly,
thanks to the Sioux and the winter. When they joined
the ragged remainder at Fort Clatsop, it was hard to say
which of them was worse off. So many casualties —
John Day and all the rest. And then came the war
of 1812, The Scots handed over the keys, and Astoria,
such as it was, became Fort George. Afterward,
Mr. Astor got some beaver, but had to share
with the Hudson Bay Company after all.

Between bad choices and bad luck,
it's amazing to think that Astoria ever happened at all.
Now, sitting here at ease, out of all danger except
that which accompanies every day alive, we sip,
and we ask: so what did they really expect?
Of course the beavers bit back.

DARK RIVER

Thanks to the isolation of the North Pacific Coast of North America, the Columbia was among the last major rivers to be mapped and explored. Its headwaters, high in Canada, confused explorers for decades, flowing in a direction seemingly opposite to its eventual course. Two-fifths of the river is in Canada, and relatively isolated. Early explorers in the late 1700s and mariners forever after were daunted by the fearsome Columbia Bar and the area's reputation as "Graveyard of the Pacific," where hundreds of ships and their crews have perished over the years.

Spring Comes to Altoona

This is the one when we head out Altoona Road
every year, a bright sunny day at spring's front door.
Could be as early as February, as late as April.
It'll likely be nippy, or maybe hot by the water, sparkling
like so many stars all set on strobe. Rafts of scaups
all splash, one for every spark.

This is the sharp corner where Deep River
and Gray's River step into the Great River together,
making Gray's Bay, making the Columbia
nine miles wide. You can just make out
the bridge, and in a few months the fireworks
will piffle downriver over Astoria. But

this is the one when fireworks come
as indecent cerise explosions of blood currant,
in the gorgets of attending hummingbirds, in
the unbearably blue wings of echo azures,
first on the wing. Altoona faces due southwest,
catches the sun full-face as soon as it tips this way.

This is the reason for this annual escapade
among the ivy-hung cliffs of basalt, the other cliffs
of mineral mud where bandtails come to lick,
in shadows of broken stacks from Pillar Rock
all the way down to here. Spring comes first
to Altoona, everyone knows that.

This is the one when we come to pay our vernal tribute.

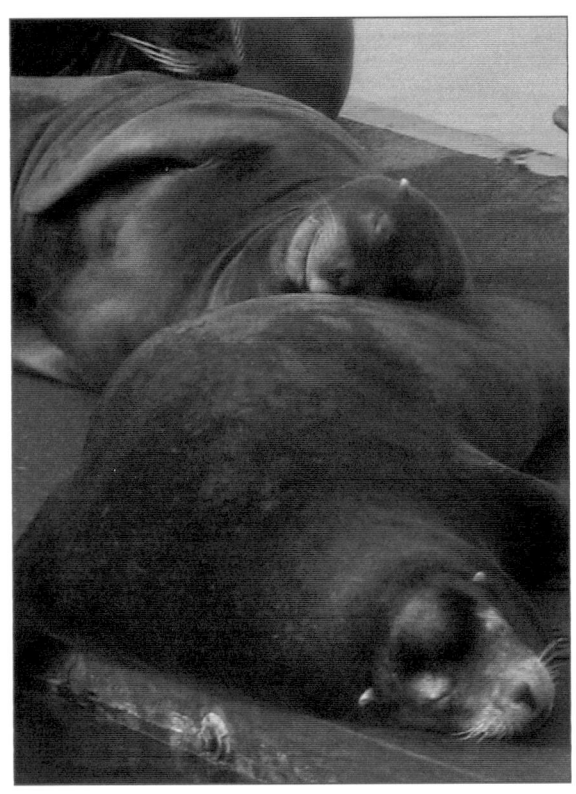

River Monsters

Lake monsters, like Nessie, Ogopogo, and Champ,
rear their heads in the form of sinker logs, looping
otters, rafts of mergansers in the fog, and maybe sometimes,
random fins of plesiosaurs.

It's the mergansers that gulled a watcher at Loch Ness
in one famous encounter (Scots call them goosanders).
Once upon Loch Ness at Castle Urquhart, I beheld
the goosanders—lined up as prescribed, dipping and diving,
only needed fog. I could see it.

Here on the big river? Oh, we've got the otters,
the mergs, and plenty of loopy lions rampant
on the whitecaps. But mostly our monsters
are logs — waterlogged sinkers, slinking
out of the murk, rearing back, and roaring
silently into the river mist their very name
which no one yet has ever heard.

ROILING WATERS

Controversies have consistently marked the historic development of the Columbia River. Often these involve divisions of ownership and responsibility across its vast historical and geographic footprint. From the loss of traditional Indian fishing grounds to federal investment in huge reclamation and power projects; from international treaty relationships with Canada to squabbles among economic, recreational, and conservation interests, the Columbia is host to man-made political, social and economic turbulence every bit as mighty as its natural power.

ROOTS

Like river pilings and other man-made features, the natural flora of the Lower Columbia have adapted remarkably to the extremes of tides, river flows, and weather. The Lewis and Clark National Wildlife Refuge and other preserved portions of the river offer access to these rare environments, known as part of the "estuary eco-system." Natural adaptations include vast swamps of Sitka Spruce which have flourished for centuries in the hybrid environment of fresh and salt water, high and low tides. Dense thickets of coast willow, Sitka willow, twinberry, osier dogwood, and Nootka rose line the channels along with abundant sedges, wildflowers, and bulrushes.

River Pubs: At the Duck

The nocturnal people of Skamokawa,
they're good eaters, occupy their chairs and bar stools
with authority. They drink, they laugh, they go
out onto the riverside porch to smoke.
Their dreams may be diminished,
but they dance for all that, drink beneath the plastic
Christmas lights, and their karaoke is much better
than you ever thought.

TV in every corner plays Animal Planet, Fox News,
sports, and weather. The waitress sets up pool balls
as a Jimmy Buffett with a belly and a voice sings out
from four lonely days in a brown L.A. haze, and the DJ,
who sings every other song, is the Walrus. Such
is night life along the river,
on the other side of K-M Mountain,
and the halibut is good.

Goodnight to the Gillnetters

On January 12, 2013 the Washington Fish and Wildlife Commission voted 7-0 to phase out gillnetting on the main-stem Columbia River. The Oregon Fish and Wildlife Commission soon followed suit, and both governors agreed.

• • •

And so we go drifting at fishdark. Remember us.
~ *Irene Martin,* Legacy and Testament

And so it comes to this.
A hundred years and half again
these small sleek craft have plied
the river's swells and rolls,
cast their nets at fishdark, to drift
the drifts their fathers knew
and theirs before, as moon or sun
or mostly rainy gray rode shotgun;
crossed the current, doubled back
then reeled the nets and pulled the catch
if any catch there was to pull;
and then went home and dried the nets
and fixed the nets and tickled the engine
and paid some bills or put them off
and then put in and did it all again,
as tides and openings allowed. This

county's forests gone to pulp,
the dairies nearly gone as well. And
yet the fishers persevere, their low-sterned
wooden boats still growl their way
from slip to drift to runways known by heart
by man and boat from all these years
of making life in town and home by taking
precious life in turn. All life means taking
life to live, and this hard-working life still
works! These fishing-family lives still work.

Or did, but now it comes to this: the thud
of gasoline motor stilled, the whap of wave
on bow and stern but echoes off a faded
chart. Wake gone slack, the cork and lead lines
all reeled in, their drums at rest, these boats bob
lonely on their last ebb tide, as darkness swamps
the river night, and all the navigation lights
(no more to pick out salmon shine) just flicker,
and go out.

People!

This isn't Wynken, Blynken, and Nod
we're talking about, who sailed off
in a wooden shoe one night to fish for
the herring fish on a river of crystal light!
These are real people with real names,
and nets of twine and nylon, not silver
and gold. Names like Haven, Stephan,
Goodell, and Crouse; Tarabochia, Clark,
and Souvenir; like Emery and Bond,
Martin and Holland, Bergseng, Backman,
Budnick, and Blix; like Stanley, McKinley,
Kuller, and Quigley, Pedersen, Olsen,
and Ostling. And these are just the ones
still here, still willing,
on Wahkiakum's docks alone.

At least thirty families, in just one county
of four thousand souls! How many more,
up and down the river? A gillnetter I know,
sick at heart, calls it rural genocide, and I
can't call him wrong, when the salmon go
for city sport instead of family jobs. This
was one place where eating close to home
made sense, supporting local people,
and the fish, dams willing, came back.

Listen! you governors of men, commissioners
of fish, you wreckers of the good and ancient ways:
How dare you steal this commonwealth
of water, land, and man, this comity of people,
fish, and river? How dare you?

And this I'd like to know as well: how
will you show your faces downstream,
when the faces of the fisherfolk
turn away?

New Year's Eve on Puget Island

Pocket-handkerchief of shoreline on the channel side.
Spruced-up, also dogwood- and blackberry-bound,
plus willow, alder, reed canary grass, and broom —
almost impenetrable.

Nearby shore rip-rapped, but green and soiled-over,
rocks filled in with volcanic ash. Sharp-shinned hawk,
breast herringboned red, swoops along the shore.
Fifty pintails rise off the river, turn north, overhead.
The sharpie shoots back across the other way,
flicking its tail like a cat. Follow it to willow cove

henged in by driftwood logs and root wads,
 platforms for gathering river silt, for growing
of sedges, shelf-fungus fingernails,
brush, briar, algae, moss, and ferns.

As if, having lost their own lives, the best
these logs and wads can do is give a boost
for something else that still wants to live.

CORMORANT

Despite loss of habitat and diminishing populations, wildlife still flourish in parts of the Lower Columbia, including the double-crested cormorant, originally described by Meriwether Lewis:

The cormorant is a large black duck which feeds on fish; I perceive no difference between it and those found in the Potomac and other rivers on the Atlantic Coast. tho' I do not recollect seeing those on the atlantic so high up the rivers as those are found here. we first met with them on the Kooskooske at the entrance of Chopunnish river. they increased in quantity as we decended, and formed much the greatest portion of the waterfowl which we saw on the Columbia untill we reached tidewater where they also abound but do not bear a similar proportion to the other fowls found in this quarter.

BASALT GEOLOGY

The Columbia is a textbook for geologists, its prehistoric course having been disarranged first by lava flows and later by ice sheets. The ice sheets were instrumental in creating the Channeled Scablands, lava flows scoured by water, exposing pre-historic rock, as well as a a series of catastrophic floods first chronicled by geologist J. Harlan Bretz. In its last stretch the river has carved the spectacular Columbia River Gorge through the Cascade Range. The river frequently reveals columnar basalt formed into spectacular pillars and monuments.

When Sam McKinney Put Out from Kelley Point

He was a riverman, if anyone ever was a riverman.
Built boats, lots of them, by hand. Took them down
the river with a relaxed grip on the wheel, a pipe
in his teeth, between a grin of sheer content.
Once he took the 16-foot *Gander* downstream
to Frankfort, ghost town above Megler, where
he spent his first summer away from home.
Another time, Sam in *Nutshell*, Robin Cody in *Turtle*,
putted up Gray's River to the head of tidewater.
When we came for them, both boats lay grounded
in the silt at low tide. Made for a nice long visit!

Later years, Sam wrote book after book —
Captain Bligh, Inside Passage, mostly Columbia.
If a man and a river ever ran together, it was
Sam McKinney and the Great River of the West.
So when he tied up his line for the last time,
what to do?

All his friends who owned a boat built by Sam
motored them down to Kelley Point Park
in North Portland. Other friends who just loved him
came too, raised a glass, told stories without end.
After the beer and all the fine words, we passed around
a bailer. Everyone took a handful of Sam, and flung
him into the wind and onto the whitecaps
at this point
where the Willamette and the Columbia meet.
And the river, and the riverman, were finally one.

SQUATTERS

Sea lions congregate on docks in various river towns like Rainier, where their barking and baying echoes among the old buildings. Animal life was abundant and varied prior to white settlement, including great runs of salmon and steelhead trout; populations of beavers, deer, elk, bears, and mountain lions; flocks of waterfowl and upland birds, including eagles, ospreys, hawks, and falcons; and many species of amphibians. The river's ability to sustain large populations of wildlife has been drastically reduced, especially for salmon and beavers. Bald eagles and peregrine falcons were once listed as endangered but have recovered in numbers throughout the region.

Road to the River

Turn down any lane off the 14, 4, or 30.
Drive as far as you can. When you hit a fence
or the end of the track, get out and walk.
Keep walking.
You'll smell it first, as the onshore wind freshens.
Smell of mud and crayfish shells, fish,
otter spraint, and rot.
Don't stop walking.
Don't stop until your feet get wet.
And then, why, you'd better stop.

A River and Its Mountains

Just because they got here when they did
Vancouver and the others "named" these snow-cones
as if they didn't have perfectly good names already.
PahTo became Adams, for a president. LooWit
transfigured to St. Helens, for a British baron.
Her other lover across the river, Wy'east, morphed
into Mt. Hood, for an English admiral.

But now, when you're coming down the river
or watching from Stonehenge at Maryhill
or gazing back up-gorge from Crown Point,
and all these cones and humps assert
their ashen presences high above the flood,
it doesn't really matter what we call them,
as if they — or their river — ever cared.

Part Four

Ebb

The change from high to low tide is the *ebb tide*. Among the least spectacular and gradual of all the tidal effects, it may have the most metaphorical familiarity: ebb tides, ebbing fortunes, at low ebb, ebb and flow. Ebb tides occur twice each lunar day, so their typical period is slightly over six hours. Ironically ebb tides may wreak as much, or more, havoc than surging springs: stranding boats, disrupting shipping channels, opening tempting mudflats, shoals and tidelands to careless explorers — and then all too soon leaving them flooded and water-bound.

HISTORIC FOG

The recent history of the Lower Columbia is particularly scant and mutable. The two states bordering the river are half the age of their eastern peers. The rugged topography has impacted navigation, settlement, and precise historiography. Even the particulars of the Lewis and Clark Expedition, the legendary Voyage of Discovery, grew hazy as the Corps approached the mouth of the Columbia, and have been subject to debate and revision.

SKELETONS

The ocean approaches to the Columbia — and indeed to much of the entire Pacific Northwest coast — are well-known in folklore as the mighty Pacific's graveyard. Unpredictable weather conditions, fog and coastal characteristics such as shifting sandbars, tidal rips, rocky reefs and shorelines have claimed more than 2,000 vessels and 700 lives near the Columbia Bar alone. Although major wrecks have declined since the 1920s, several lives are still lost annually. The lethal combination of fog, wind, storm, current and wave wreaked havoc through the middle of the twentieth century, leaving wrecks made famous in regional history and skeletons still visible today.

Once Upon Brookfield

This northern shore was packed with fishing towns,
canneries thick as sea-lice on a spawned-out silver hen.
Skamokawa to Baker Bay, palaces of red boards arose
to slime, cut, and can the millions of salmon
from fish-trap, wheel, horse-seiner, or boat. Towns,
to house the Finnish fishers and Chinese canners.
Graced with post offices, stores, schools, even
telephone lines, they grew out of the wilderness
'twixt high tides and high firs. Bosses' mansions
looked down on raw new streets, hopeful spokes
of human longing and desire. Megler, Knappton,
Frankfort, Altoona, Cottardi, Dahlia, Pillar Rock...
and chief among them, beautiful Brookfield.

Brookfield began in 1873 with a cannery manned
by Croatian fishermen. Occupied a pretty bay
between Harrows Creek and Brookfield Point.
No roads, only mail-boats, until log trucks came.
Soon the old-growth ran out, both in river and hills.
Cannery abandoned, steamers didn't stop any more.
School closed in '45, P.O. in '53. In '57, Crown
Zellerbach bulldozed the town, and that was that.

We used to pore over foundations, pick through
moss and ivy-strewn paths among the giveaway
daffodils and snowdrops, looking for signs: shards
of blue willow ware, keys, an old toy, a marble;
rusted stove here, broken front steps over there.
Imagining lives once lived, loves long gone. You
can still get to Brookfield, through the logged-
off hills. But all you'll see is dredge spoils
and stumps, and the only signs on the forest floor
are the shiny ones left by slugs and snails.

I Cross the Columbia

How many times have I crossed this river?
Five hundred? A thousand? First time,
1964, with my mother, bringing me by rail
from Colorado to see her beloved Northwest.
It took. So there were many crossings to come
on the *Portland Rose*, the *City of Portland*, and
eventually Amtrak, or sometimes Greyhound,
Seattle to Denver and back again. Later,
in a dynasty of Volkswagens, it was I-5 and 205,
the Bridge of the Gods, Hood River, The Dalles,
Biggs, Umatilla, Vernita, and Vantage: for jobs,
field trips, family, all the reasons one has
for changing states of being. When I moved
downstream to a lower trib, crossings shifted
to the Lewis & Clark in Longview, the ferry
at Westport, in Honda, Toyota, Subaru.
Now I cross the river more than ever before —
at Megler, the last bridge before the bar,
And gladly so! For when I cross the Columbia now,
I am crossing it to you.

A DIFFERENT KIND OF FLOW

To motorists, sportsmen and tourists, they are impressive, monolithic structures that add a colossal dimension to the river flowing among them. And to academics, geologists and historians, they are equally impressive: The Columbia River Flood Basalts are one of the youngest and best preserved continental flood basalt provinces on earth. These monumental rock formations are one of at least three flows that have formed the region: extensive eruptions and lava flows; crushing flows of ice and dammed ice water suddenly loose over the land; and, of course, the more benevolent flows of water that still sculpt and shape the land to this day.

BOOMS AND RAFTS

The Columbia serves as a highway for all kinds of travelers, including logs on their way to the sawmill or for shipment overseas. Originally, "log drivers" wrestled individual logs downstream, an extremely dangerous practice. Bundling lots into larger rafts — some of enormous size, as much as 2,000 feet long — gave them stability and allowed them to be towed and maneuvered. Log booms, on the other hand, were stationary, and anchored by several logs driven as pilings to catch logs directed their way. Though they look similar, the boom remains in place while the raft travels the waterway.

Christmas on the Columbia

Anyone who doesn't know the river
might think it's lit up for the holidays
year round, all those red and green directional buoys
flashing "go here, not there," up and down the reach.
Colors of holly leaf and berry borrowed
from solstices in Druid days, representing
Yuletide in these forgetful times.
But sometime after Thanksgiving
(that other pagan holdover) other brilliants appear —
red and green, yes, bus also blue and gold and white —
all along the river's shores. Line
doorways and window frames, parade
through marinas and backwaters on festive boats,
their lit-up lines reflecting shapes of Christmas trees.

Elk and deer are brought home from the hunt,
turkeys from Freddies's for feasts ashore
or adrift. Children visit Santas at Grange Hall and mall.
Carols lap at pilings, old chestnuts sung in voices
muted by waves and rain.

Such are the midwinter rites and revels on the river,
where a long wet night will take whatever it can get
to hold back the dark — even if it's only
"go here, not there," blinking red and green,
all up and down the reach.

Small Craft Advisory

Marinas all along the river house
small craft, docked overnight, overwinter,
or forever, in slips along the patient docks.
You can't help walking these floating gangways
looking for the boat that wants you. Or try
to ignore the ones with dim lights aglow —
the liveaboards, the overnighters. You have to wonder:
what are they getting up to in there?

The sailboats especially, but also tugs,
old wooden cruisers, lesser yachts, tiny
makeshift houseboats, even the big
crass stinkpots. You wonder too, isn't
there something there to envy after all?
And could you live like that? Letting the river
make up your mind, where to go, what to do,
besides listen to weather radio and plot charts?

Could anything be so cozy — or so dank?
But watch out: it could be catching.

Dredge Spoils

And so the manufactured islands and beaches grow
from sand scraped out for ships and spewed
from the gullets of dredges, onto new shores.

Valuable, to build beaches against the wakes of ships,
protect the houses of Sunny Shores, while deepening
the channel for commerce up and down the river of return.

Downright useful, too, for all the plants and creatures
that come to lodge upon their gritty mounds. Cormorants
and Caspian terns, horned larks and hellebores.

Whole islands straddle the state line
that were not there before. Once I convinced my kids
that Washington and Oregon fought a war over them

and that wasn't far off: Sand Island attracted the Marines
on one side, the National Guard on the other,
though neither state has made much use of it since.

These islands are "spoils" more like booty, than ruined,
from the animals' standpoint. How funny that a word can mean
its own opposite, like sanction, cleave, or spoil.

How strong the urge of life
to make every inch of habitat count
for all it's worth.

Two Rivers

Two rivers run down to the bay, meeting at Miller Point.
One short, all tidal, and deep, like its name.
One long, from the hills, tidal just to the town of its name,
and many days gray, just like its name.
Two snaky bodies of water, making their beds between forest and field,
looking to find their way, together.

Past ghost towns of the Finns and the Swedes.
Past log dumps and stumps of forests past.
Past the churches and creameries and graveyards and stores.
Past wood ducks, and otters, muskrats and mink.
Two snaky bodies of water, making their beds between forest and field,
looking to find their way, together.

Two rivers rush down to the bay
under bridges and raindrops and roads,
through gorges and culverts and tidegates,
By docks and houses, gillnets and mudbanks.
By kingfishers, eagles, reedgrass, and newts.
Ospreys, salmon, suckers and smelt.
Past meadows of cattle and elk,
shadows of cedars and spruce,
all the way to the bay, the big river, the bar,
all the way to the sea.

These rivers are rolling...
these rivers are rocking on down...

Two snaky bodies of water,
finding their way, together.

MARITIME

Most of the Lower Columbia and tidewater reach enjoy a classic maritime climate, with the occasional interruption of severe Pacific storms. Average annual high temperatures are in the high 50s, lows in the low 40s, and averages a comfortable 50 degrees. Precipitation, which tends to fall as drizzle as much as downpour, is another story: an average of some 50-plus inches of rain a year, climbing to 80-plus inches in Astoria, and as much as 120 inches annually in Grays River. As for the relatively low probability phenomenon known as snow: about 1-2 inches a year.

What the Muskrat Saw

slipping through the marsh beneath the striders
as the beaver, ten times his size, slid through the pond
beside the dam where aspen lay akimbo, stripped
of bark above the runnel where the rainbow rose
to meet the hatch of caddis at the riffle
of the kingfisher's rattle through the willow's shadow
on the river where the cottonwood leaf floated
over sandy bottoms scored with crayfish holes
and rocks all coated with snails, whose tentacles quivered
at the passage of the blennies and the scissor of the heron's bill
which came up empty for a change because the mink disturbed
the fish a moment early and they in turn alarmed a frog that leapt
upon a fallen log where otter sunned before returning
upstream to the marsh where the muskrat, slipping
underneath the striders, saw him, and rose
into his reedy house.

Ceremony

The road kill was black, long, red at one end — a vulture?
Went back to look. My god, it's a bear! A tiny bear, tumped
up against the guard rail. Eighteen inches, maybe ten pounds
tops. Smaller than my cat, certainly skinnier. A tiny teddy:
head crushed, that's why the red. Sad, shocked, toss
him into the brush. Better, anyway, than hard asphalt.

But it doesn't sit right, like I haven't done right by the bear.
Some ceremony? A better, softer resting place? Go back today.
Heavy, brambly scramble down steep slope through cans
and plastic, ferns and firs, rotting branches. Hang onto sword fern
with its napthalene smell, hang over punji stakes of alder slash,
back and forth across that no-man's land between highway and life.
No sign; guess the coyotes took him already. Then, down final slope,
the bear — shiny fur, like acrylic in the sun, hung up in salal.

So I lift him — he's a little boy — by a paw. Less than a bag of sugar.
Farther down, mossy maple sticks out toward river. Teddies belong
on beds, says the little boy in me. Cinch way out the broad trunk, lay
little bear on his tummy on the bole. Stuff his busted jaw back in,
close his mouth with moss, lay paw over rubbery snout, the way my
cat likes to sleep. Feel those long, half-circle claws, thick and sharp;
those soft, cool pads like an old man's feet wrinkled by the rain.
Run my fingers through the soft fur that clothes that baby's body,
dry now, silky, warm in the evening sun.

Then clamber back up to the road, and down again, with four
long wands of false Solomon's seal, fragrant as orange blossom.
Squinch out the trunk again to lay the creamy racemes
around that shattered little head, you'd never know.
Say some words for the bear; for the world. Tug once more
his velvet elfin ears, turn, jump down, and go. Feel better now.

But later, over wine, I have to ask: who was it all for?
Some spirit bear? I don't think so. For the little bear?
A bear is just a bear, and the bear didn't care. Raven
watched the proceedings, and tomorrow the vultures will visit,
flowers scatter, little bear go back. So again I ask, who was it for?

For whom did I play "The Ballad of Frankie Lee and Judas Priest"
at my brother's funeral, lay new cottonwood shoots on his beautiful
cottonwood box? And for whom did I wash my own love's body,
dress her in soft white cotton, and flowers?

BOAT CRADLE

Located on the waterfront near the Astoria-Megler Bridge, this decaying boat cradle is among the last in the region. Designed to ramp a boat up and down into the river, it's a variation on a device ubiquitous among mariners — usually employed to either lift, travel with, or store a boat. Just as it sounds, rather than enfolding the boat the cradle simply provides a form-fitting resting place, with or without lifts, wheels or locomotion.

TRACKS

Bird life remains abundant in the tidewater reach. In fact, thanks to habitat we have provided, the double-crested cormorant has become super-abundant, preying on young salmon and befouling the Astoria bridge with guano. Lewis and Clark paid special attention to bird life. One accounting claims the expedition discovered and named more than 50 new species of birds, while recording the presence of 120 familiar fowl.

River Pubs: The View from Maria's

Ernesto brings a pint of Aye Aye IPA
and a brace of tongue taquitos. Outside, fugitive
sun on work-release from the constant cloudbank
skitters the river with tinsel. A minute later,
iron filings.

The railing out the window is the same color
as the bottles of Cholula and Tapatio on the table.
Beyond their red ranks, through the rain,
Wright's Hardware hulks beneath the longest
tarpaper roof in the county: admission by appointment,
call Wally; he's probably got what you need. It rests
its rangey gambrels against the biggest red camellia anywhere,
carmine blossoms fixing to rot on the wet turf alongside,
where a skirted old airboat holds up its end. Six Brusco tugs
stand ready to push from the other side, if needed.

Here's where they filmed *Snow Falling on Cedars*,
because nowhere else, Humboldt County to Juneau,
looked old enough. "If I had Wright's Hardware in Hollywood,"
said the production designer, "I could retire."
Cathlamet on the Columbia: a county seat that just sits
and sits, and shows no sign of going anywhere, very fast.

Fetching the Old Town at Scappoose

They'd made some extra money that month,
those photos from New Guinea in *Smithsonian*,
and all the bills were paid for a change. Wanting
a canoe in the worst way, they took the VW bus
and their three hundred bucks downriver to Scappoose:
"Brown's Landing," read the sign. "Boats & Canoes."

It was an Old Town of Maine that caught their eye.
Not a classic wooden one like that sleek craft
they'd paddled in the Thousand Islands that fall,
they could never afford that. So, fiberglass.
But the struts were oak and the paddles, spruce.
Eighteen foot — long for solo, but they were two —
plenty of stowage, and a keel to keep it stable.

They slipped it down the ramp into Multnomah Slough
and it felt good. So over the years, it was up and down
all those tribs, all those tidal sloughs, though almost never
the river itself, too big for an open paddle craft, for them.
The Gray's, of course, and Steamboat, Ellsworth, Elochamon;
the Deep, the Bone, Seal Slough, Teal Slough; the Bear.
The Not-Quite-Whitewater River Run, with the kids.

Eventually to Long Island and its giant cedars, where
they'd always meant to go. But by then he was solo;
plunked a chunk of oak or random kid in the bow
for ballast, to keep it from becoming a sail
when the wind came up on the inbound leg. The struts
rotted out over forty years, the cream hull scratched
by boat-launch cobbles and ninebark branches
on shore, where all those picnics and landings took place.

Nowadays, it's mostly a Grandpa Camp thing: lazing
down to tidewater, pulling hard back up again,
as long as the good lad is willing. And it is still
his pleasure sometimes to lie flat, butt on seat,
head resting on stern, feet on gunwhales; to pop
a beer, close his eyes, and drift.

Long Dock

It could be anywhere on the river
where people want to get down to the water
for all the reasons people do.
There's never been a time
when people have lived along the water
that they didn't build docks
to get to boats to ducks to damselflies
in hoop by the water's edge.
The longer the better,
since it prolongs anticipation,
puts off the moment of arrival,
when toe goes into water
or butt into boat. The docks
are the entry-points. And when
you reach the end, only two things
are possible: enter the river,
or walk back up to the longing land,
and start to long for water once more.

MOON IN FULL

For ancient people the Moon made magic: the subject of veneration, celebration, and ritual. The ancients reveled as the moon grew full, but also knew that next day's low tide would be particularly so, and made haste to their fishing or shelling grounds. The Moon embodies both change and changelessness: It was revered spiritually as a god or goddess, and consulted practically as a timekeeper and regulator.

All Fall Down

Along the river shore lies
a forest of boards, salmon-red and brown,
bobbing on the high gray tide, soaking
them a little darker than their faded state,
as if the river splintered into kindling
to feed the fire, the cold fire
of the flotsam with all that's left
of Altoona Cannery. Waves flap
at its wreckage, slapping the remnants
of broad floors whose pilings gave way
when the land's loose logs came down.
The flood that took this house of salmon
was time.

A wedge of geese flies over Megler Bridge, across
the far reach. One more old one down,
one more forest to the sea, in a land
where the sea is cheap
and all the rest is long gone.

Robert Michael Pyle and Judy VanderMaten
Cathlamet, Wash., Spring 2020

ROBERT MICHAEL PYLE

Bob Pyle is a Pacific Northwest natural resource. As a scholar, writer, naturalist and teacher, he shares his love of the natural environment with a worldwide audience. His 24 books include the Northwest classic *Wintergreen* and three prior collections of poems. A lifelong lepidopterist, he moves gracefully and purposefully, like his dear butterflies, among academics, boots-on-the-ground naturalists, and the people and places of his beloved Willapa Hills.

Bob is a Guggenheim Fellow, winner of the John Burroughs Medal for Distinguished Nature Writing, and a regular contributor to Columbia River Reader.

JUDY VANDERMATEN

Judy VanderMaten was smitten by photography as a child in her native Iowa. A Brownie Instamatic, a class in the school's darkroom, and the magic of a print materializing in her hands — and before her eyes — set her on her life's path. Careers as a teacher and exhibitor refined and defined her vision, and proximity to the Columbia River excited her passion.

Judy documents her world travels in extraordinary photographs, and returns to her Columbia River home for affirmation and inspiration.

DEBBY NEELY

Cover woodcut: "The Winter Moon."

Debby Neely is a teacher and student of graphic design enchanted by the ancient art of the woodcut. "I sign my name with the red chops. The top chop is my name in Chinese. The bottom chop says I draw birds and animals."

COLUMBIA RIVER READER PRESS

CRR Press is a subsidiary of Columbia River Reader, LLC, a regional literary and lifestyle publication headquartered in Southwest Washington State.

www.crreader.com/CRRPress

A NOTE ABOUT TYPE

The Tidewater Reach is set in Baskerville, designed by John Baskerville in Birmingham, England, in the 1750s. Baskerville changed popular type design, increasing the contrast between thick and thin strokes, sharpening and tapering the serifs, and shifting the axis of rounded letters to a more vertical position. The design was influenced by the calligraphy Baskerville had learned as a young man, and his typefaces remain popular to this day.

ACKNOWLEDGEMENTS

We wish to thank all of our neighbors in the Lower Columbia region, human and otherwise, whether mentioned in the poems or not. Vast thanks are due Sue Piper and Hal Calbom, of Columbia River Reader Press, for seeing and helping to mold our vision, and for bringing this long-sailing dreamboat safely in to port.

R.M. Pyle and Judy VanderMaten ~ Spring 2020

The poets and listeners of Ric's Poetry Mic at WineKraft in Astoria have been my ever-helpful first audience for many of these poems.

Prior publication of the following poems, and gracious permission for reprinting them here, is hereby and gratefully acknowledged:

> *Moon Museum*, Heartbreak Press: "A Moon I Didn't See"
>
> *Evolution of the Genus Iris*, Lost Horse Press: "A Moon I Didn't See," "Pencil Shavings," "Gulls at Rest," "All Fall Down"
>
> *Chinook & Chanterelle*, Lost Horse Press: "Bretz's Flood," "Duffy's Deck," "At the Duck," "Goodnight to the Gillnetters"
>
> *Butterfly Launches from Spar Pole*, Murky Slough Music: "Bretz's Flood," "The Big Wave," "Two Rivers," "Ceremony"

Thank you, Judy, for sharing this vision with me all these years and for the beauty you bring into the world through your eyes and your lens. And to my dear friend and essential poetry partner, Florence Sage, I wish to dedicate this book.

R.M.P., Gray's River, Wash.

I'd like to gratefully thank my husband, Chris Holmes, for supporting me on this project and being willing to explore river areas with me by hiking and kayaking with me.

I'd also like to thank an old friend of mine, Erik Larsson who sparked the interest in making photographs in me at a young age.

I'd also like to thank the Columbia River Keepers for connecting me with so many others who are passionate about the river and who are constantly working to keep the Columbia alive and healthy!

And a big thanks to Bob for not giving up on this project that we started several years ago.

J.V., Cathlamet, Wash.

COLUMBIA RIVER READER PRESS

We are celebrators, curators and custodians of the Lower Columbia River region of the Pacific Northwest — its history, culture, and art.

Columbia River Reader Press is a subsidiary of Columbia River Reader, a literary and lifestyle publication published monthly in Southwest Washington State. The *Reader* has steadily expanded its distribution and advertising base over the last 16 years, and in 2019 announced expansion plans which included launching Columbia River Reader Press and a yearly subscription service, the CRR Collector's Club.

The Tidewater Reach, published in two editions — a Signature Edition, in color, with artists' autographs; and a black and white, trade paperback edition — is the inaugural CRR Press publication. In the works is a compilation of the *Reader's* popular monthly feature, "Dispatches from the Discovery Trail," to be published in Autumn 2020.

CRR Press also distributes select works which amplify its mission and cater to the interests of its readers. First among these are three books by regional author Rex Ziak, who revolutionized Lewis and Clark scholarship and changed the historical record: *In Full View; Eyewitness to Astoria;* and *Down and Up the Columbia River.*

For ordering and subscription information, see the following page, or to order online using a credit card, visit www.crreader.com/crrpress.

CRR Press books are also available in custom editions, suitable for particular audiences. For additional information please contact:

Columbia River Reader Press
1333 14th Avenue
Longview, Washington 98632
email: CRRPress@crreader.com

COLUMBIA RIVER READER PRESS

COLUMBIA RIVER READER COLLECTORS CLUB

To use credit card, visit www.crreader.com/crrpress. To pay by check, please use the mail order form below.

THE TIDEWATER REACH

☐ The Tidewater Reach (Color and B/W)
Boxed Signature Edition ___ @ $50 = _____

☐ The Tidewater Reach (B/W)
Paperback edition ___ @ $25 = _____

☐ In Full View ___ @ $30 = _____

☐ Eyewitness to Astoria ___ @ $22 = _____

☐ Down and Up ___ @ $19 = _____

Add Book Shipping & Handling $ 3.90

                            Sub-Total _____

BOOKS BY REX ZIAK

☐ Columbia River Reader
11-issue Subscription ___ @ $55 = _____
Start with next issue.
For gift subscription, include name, mailing address;
announcement card will be included with first issue.

Washington residents
add sales tax   8.1%_____

CRR Press
1333 14th Ave.
Longview, WA 98632

                    TOTAL _____

*Please enclose check payable to CRR Press;
to pay via credit card, please call 360-749-1021.*

Name _____

Street _____

City/State/Zip _____

email _____

Phone _____

Here the impossible union
Of spheres of existence is actual
Here the past and future
Are conquered, and reconciled...

~ T. S. Eliot
"The Dry Salvages" (from Four Quartets)

A Conversation with Robert Michael Pyle

Hal Calbom

Robert Michael Pyle and Hal Calbom
Gray's River, Wash., February 2018

A Conversation with Robert Michael Pyle
Part One: Gray's River

The vigorous man in the flannel shirt, white beard and mudded boots looks entirely at home walking into Duffy's Irish Pub, the chief wide spot in the road in Gray's River. Over lunch and a couple of glasses of cabernet we settle down for two hours of conversation. I ask Pyle what led him to Wahkiakum County, Washington, his home now for more than 40 years.

RMP: After a drive through the hills, my field assistant and I were about to go back to Portland. I started to turn left and then I said, "Wait a minute, I remember a covered bridge near here. Let's go see it."

HRC: You were working for the Nature Conservancy? When?

RMP: Yes, from 1977 to 1980; this was August of 1978. David said, "I'm from upstate New York, I see covered bridges all the time. Let's get back to Portland for dinner." And I said, "You're a kid, I'm the boss of this car. I want to go see the covered bridge!" So we did, and that's when I saw the sign, For Sale By Owner, on the old farmhouse beneath giant oak trees. The other thing I saw was one of those broad, green valleys just like those I had idealized on a spring day back in 1970. It was the coming together of all these elements that really enchanted me.

HRC: Was the house in good shape?

RMP: Structurally it was sound, if showing all of its eighty years. The grounds had deteriorated from the virtual arboretum it once had been, which gave it the name "Swede Park." But I liked the wildness.

HRC: You mentioned that you got a second opinion?

RMP: Yes, my dad took a look and he said, "Why do you want to move out here to this rainy place? Why do you want to leave Colorado? Colorado's a paradise!" I said, "Dad, too cold in the winter, too hot in the summer," just as he had said about Ohio when he'd moved to Colorado!

Growing up near Denver, Pyle was a self-admitted shy kid enamored of the natural world. He belonged to a "Seashell of the Month" club and saved his allowance money for new selections, chased butterflies, and threw the discus on the track team. His initial attraction to the Pacific Northwest? Marine biology, not butterflies. His college of choice? The University of Washington.

RMP: I say in *Wintergreen*, in the philosophical chapter called "And the Coyotes Will Lift a Leg," that everybody's invited to serendipity's picnic but you've got to accept the invitation…to be aware, and to act. Will I admit to being an opportunist? I hope not in the negative sense of taking advantage of people, but I was aware of some remarkable and lucky opportunities, and I took them.

HRC: And those opportunities included a Fulbright and a Ph.D. from Yale? Not bad for a failed discus thrower.

RMP: Well, I did letter in track, but I was way too small to fling the platter in college. But yes, these things help. As for the Ph.D. it has allowed me to cash checks in strange towns! If I were a fatalist who talked about things being meant to happen, you could find lots of such places in my story. But I prefer Jung's hypothesis of "the physics of fate," which says that there's so damn much going on all the time that you are bound to have serendipity if you pay attention to what's around you.

HRC: And you became aware of here?

RMP: Yes! On that butterfly field trip. We'd come across to Wahkiakum because it was the one county in Washington for which I had no butterfly data. I had done my doctorate at Yale based on analysis of Washington butterfly distribution, comparing it against nature reserve distribution to see what the butterflies could tell us about gaps in the conservation system. But nobody told me it rains here all the time and there aren't any butterflies! Well, there are, but it's taken a while to find them.

HRC: You've managed to do pretty well for being in the wrong place at the wrong time.

RMP: Gray's River has really been very much the right place at the right time for me — all forty-two years now. I've isolated myself to some degree. I've rusticated. Oh, I'm involved in the community, but not nearly as much as some of my friends. The fact that you've got this barreling rain, 120 to 150 inches of it, and a lot of days that are just not inviting to get out into the world very much, definitely helps one make the transition into sitting down and writing. The books take a lot of time, and the rain helps keep me at it.

Robert Michael Pyle is among Washington's most prolific and highly regarded authors. His notable books include Wintergreen; Where Bigfoot Walks: Crossing the Dark Divide; Sky Time in Grays River; *and* The Tangled Bank, *a collection of essays. He is both careful observer and grand expounder, a powerful combination: a magician of the rain and wet weather who transforms a walk out to the compost pile into an odyssey, and talks to loggers as easily as lepidopterists.*

RMP: With *Wintergreen*, I transitioned from an urban conservationist who thought logging was bad to understanding something about a rural community and its jobs. Mind you, I had only lived here eight years — to write such a book so soon is kind of rude, because I criticized some of their practices. But I also made a case for better practices that would respect the people of the woods as well as the woods, and for sustainable forestry over the long term. How could I be anti-logging? I came out of two forestry schools, and I know where the pulp for my books comes from. Once a couple of loggers came to my house in their stagged-off jeans, cork boots, and red suspenders. At least they'd left their chainsaws in their rig, a good sign. "You that guy Powell?" They called me "Powell," you know?

HRC: Trouble?

RMP: "You write that book 'Evergreen'?" They called it "Evergreen." I said, "Yeah, I guess so." "Well, we want to buy a couple of copies and have you sign 'em." Because they got it! They got that I was criticizing short-term corporate logging practices that hurt their families as well as the forest.

HRC: Are you primarily a West Side guy, west of the Cascades, or do you range farther afield?

RMP: My natural habitat is the green and the moist. But I do love the east side too. The dry slope is richer in butterflies, particularly in the mountain canyons. I do enjoy going over there just to immerse myself in those sweaty canyons or desert steppes. I go to a special place in Asotin County where the Grande Ronde River flows into the Snake River. I found one new butterfly for Washington there, and I'm on the trail of another one. I do love eastern Washington, but I am always happy to get back to the damp.

HRC: Are these echoes of your Colorado upbringing, or a completely new scene set?

RMP: West side and east side speak to different parts of me, and both loves come from my childhood. My mother, born in Seattle, and her mother, a pioneer teacher, always spoke of rain and ferns and moss. Those stories drew me here. But the east side speaks to what I imprinted on as a kid in Colorado, grasslands and desert and heat and sage. *The Thunder Tree* is my "dry book," as *Wintergreen* is my "wet book." Washingtonians are very fortunate to have easy access to both of these worlds.

HRC: As a truly amateur geologist but professional filmmaker I love the drama of the landscapes, the coulees, the Channeled Scablands.

RMP: As you know, it was the Glacial Lake Missoula Floods that carved out those landforms. J. Harlan Bretz was ridiculed when he pointed this out, but now we call them the Bretz Floods. That is the title of one of the song-poems I've composed and perform with Krist Novoselić and Ray Prestegard on our album

Butterfly Launches from Spar Pole (butterflylaunch.com). It celebrates that great green gouge, the epic carving of the gorge that permitted the free transit of water all the way from the Pend Oreille country to Ilwaco — at least until the dams — and imbued the Columbia with much of its magic to this day.

HRC: We're about eight to ten miles from the Columbia, up the Grays River? Does the magic extend up here?

RMP: Oh, yes! When the American seafarer Robert Gray came in May 1792, ultimately depriving us of Canadian health insurance because he beat Vancouver over the bar, his name stuck. This place was hopping a hundred years ago. It's been all downhill ever since, economically. And yet something special persists. Thank the gods we are beyond the commuter zone. Relative isolation and rain keep the population blessedly low: four thousand! No traffic lights in the whole county.

HRC: Are you here to escape from human beings? Urban life?

RMP: Urban life, yes; I've got little use for it. But people, no. I enjoy the kind folks here. I really came to encounter nature daily, including people. Among these fields, forests, and rivers, I'll never be bored.

Pyle is concerned over climate change, loss of habitat, conservation of public lands. However, as I learned in our conversation, he's also empathetic and realistic. His one axe to grind — sitting here in the heart of timber country — is with those who would separate the provinces of man and nature. He calls it dualism.

RMP: Any world view that objectifies the other, attempts to dominate the other. A duality between humans and nature is the most dangerous idea there is. Everything I write tries to smear that false line, which licenses all manner of enormities against the non-human world, the more-than-human world. The Willapa Hills are as good a place as any to work on reconciling people as a part of nature.

HRC: You have called yourself an urban conservationist.

RMP: That was me when I lived in the city, working to save bits and pieces of urban habitat. Now I work to reconcile country and city attitudes, as an urban/rural dualism is dangerous too. Many local people see the liberal cities as the tail wagging the dog, imposing values and regulations that just don't fit here. I don't go along with general blackballing of the city. But I will say that it's easy to be an urban conservationist who discounts rural needs.

HRC: I think of the line from William Blake, "Without man, nature is barren."

RMP: I don't fully agree with Blake there. Nature will outlast us, of course, and be just fine. But the inverse certainly applies: Without the rest of nature, humans aren't just barren — they're toast.

HRC: One of the prominent listings in your bio is "founder of the Xerces Society." Which is?

RMP: My Fulbright Scholarship to England was to study butterfly conservation in the only place it was being much done. I founded Xerces (named for the extinct Xerces Blue butterfly) in 1971, as a means of applying what I had learned. Now the Xerces Society for Invertebrate Conservation has more than 50 staff in five states, and is the largest pollinator conservation team in the world. I am very proud of them. Based in Portland, they work all over to protect "the little things that run the world," as Xerces' former president E.O. Wilson called the insects.

HRC: What's on your agenda now? Works in progress?

RMP: My first novel, *Magdalena Mountain*, set in my native Colorado, came out in 2018 from Counterpoint Press. I worked on that forty-four years, wrote ten drafts. Now I am working on a sequel to be called *The Silver Satyr*, which will take place mostly in the Andes. But I think I'll have to write it a lot faster this time. My collection *Nature Matrix: New and Selected Essays* comes out in autumn 2020. And a feature film *The Dark Divide*, based on my book *Where Bigfoot Walks*, is about to be released. I am played by the remarkable actor David Cross.

HRC: I think of you as a non-fiction guy?

RMP: I read more fiction than non-fiction. I find the two inform each other — and writing fiction is fun!

HRC: And, some poems, I understand?

RMP: Yes, many poems. Poetry is at the heart of my current writing. I have two published collections and a third at press, called *The Last Man in Willapa*. And of course now comes *The Tidewater Reach*, my poems with the stunning images of Cathlamet photographer Judy VanderMaten. It is our love song to the estuary of the Great River of the West.

HRC: I can't tell you how much I've enjoyed this.

RMP: Are you going to eat that last oyster? I'll trade you a river poem for it.

HRC: Deal.

RMP: Watching the river otters' sleek and pointy loop-de-loop
                over and over and over
                I managed to miss the evening news.

(continued page 178)

Robert Michael Pyle and Judy VanderMaten
Cathlamet, Wash., March 2020

A Conversation with Robert Michael Pyle
Part Two: Cathlamet

Robert Michael Pyle succeeded in finding a publisher, Columbia River Reader Press, for his collaboration with photographer Judy VanderMaten. Their book, The Tidewater Reach, *combines forty-four of Pyle's poems with color and black and white photos by VanderMaten, all focused on the Lower Columbia River region, "the reach" where tidal salt water and fresh river water intermingle.*

RMP: When I first envisioned *The Tidewater Reach*, I assumed my contribution would be in prose, like most of my books.

HRC: What changed your mind? What attracted you to poetry?

RMP: Over the last couple of years I've written and performed and published more and more poetry, and I came to realize its special attractions and capabilities. First of all is brevity. While many readers will pass by an essay because of the time it takes to read, they can enjoy any of these poems in a minute or two or a few.

HRC: Ironic that poetry, which is thought to be so esoteric, would actually suit our notoriously short attention spans.

RMP: Yes, that concision. That focus. It also allows me to engage many more subjects and changes of scene than I readily could have done with prose. Not that it takes any less time to write and refine a good poem, but you can get your ideas and inspirations down quickly, on the ferry, in a pub, or over a glass of wine; then come back to edit, re-write, and flesh out the poem later. Poetry is much like *plein-air* painting that way, and this makes it a rich medium for taut, memorable description of scenes and action.

HRC: So this is both a liberation and a bit of a discipline, too?

RMP: Oh, very much so. Instead of going on and on, you cut to the heart of the matter, and realize that concision is its own reward.

HRC: Do you write for the voice or the page?

RMP: Both. I do numerous readings of poems and enjoy them. But of course I publish in print. Poetry sings to us. Every poem is a song — lyric — but usually spoken rather than following melody. While prose has its rhythm for sure, lyrical poetry lives in its cadence whether formal or free verse. By laying out your thoughts, images, and revelations in lines, rather than paragraphs or sentences, you may omit extraneous words and structure and lathe the song right down to its essence.

HRC: You also tell stories in your poems. They're not just lyrics.

RMP: Certainly. Many of my poems are stories that relate to the readers' own experience, and as such, are very accessible — definitely not esoteric. Still, why not tell them in conventional prose? Because the line breaks mean as much as the words themselves, indicating natural pauses and flow in the song; and the ability to take liberties with grammar or syntax in favor of narrative means that the poet can concentrate on bewitchment instead of mere structure.

HRC: Ah, bewitchment. And the power of voice. Casting spells.

RMP: Sure. "The Book Boat" is a fable that could also be told in prose, but placing it in verse lets me select and emphasize certain words, phrases and physical elements such that the attentive reader makes a novel out of a two-page poem. A good essay is a fine thing, but a good poem will stick to your ribs — and to the heart within.

Publishing* The Tidewater Reach *culminates almost twenty years nursing, developing, and shopping the project. Or, to be more precise, "querying," in the words of the poet himself. For editor and publisher, as well as the author and photographer, pairing poems and pictures — and giving each their due, their evocative relationship one with the other — was substantially more difficult than they first imagined and required careful attention and thought.

HRC: Do the pictures lead the poems, or vice versa?

RMP: It's an intricate relationship. Neither the pictures nor the poems can be said to "lead." Certainly Judy and I were inspired by many of the same things, and I was directly inspired by some of the photographs.

HRC: Are the poems captions or commentaries for the photographs?

RMP: Definitely not. In a lot of photography books the words are window dressing for the pictures, secondary or even throwaway. We didn't want that, or the reverse. In our book the pictures and the poems are presented on an equal footing, to expand the reader / looker's view of one another. We believe the whole really is greater than the sum of the parts.

HRC: But you've said you're wary of the other extreme: that full-blown essays might simply be too much?

RMP: It's a lot to ask of readers in an age of diminishing attention spans. I decided it would be too damned much work to write thirty essays if few people would read them. Plus I've written so much prose about the Columbia. I certainly didn't want to reiterate *Wintergreen* or *Sky Time*.

HRC: And, a change of pace? Of medium?

RMP: Yes. I finally decided if we were going to do this thing then I was darned well going to make it fun. I wanted to write whole-heartedly, and what I'm really enjoying now is poetry.

HRC: Does poetry suffer from a bad rap? There seem to be people who claim to simply not get it. Or that it's obscure, pretentious?

RMP: Yes, poetry does suffer in the public mind. I think this is because most folks were taught archaic, formal poems in school that had nothing to do with their own experience. They think of poetry as a different, rather unpleasant language. Pretentious and obscure, yes, but also just too much work to bother with. We know that contemporary poetry doesn't have to be that way, and in fact can be fun. Of course it takes real attention to properly appreciate a photograph too, but people can just look at them if they wish, while a poem must be actually read. Sure, some people will buy the book for the pictures and never read the poems. But if they'll just give them a try, and dive into the playful language, stories, and rich natural images, they just might get hooked

HRC: It seems like you've worked hard to make these accessible?

RMP: I didn't really have to work at it. My poems are accessible, because they arise from real-life stories, impressions of the familiar world, and ordinary language: things we all know. The pictures will help open the way for the poetry, and vice versa. Once readers get into the poems, I guarantee they're not going to be intimidated by them.

Bob Pyle's work transcends genre and region. His voyages seem migratory, like the butterflies he so loves. Yet, at the same time, he reveres a sense of place, and the intimate details of places. Recently his name has been attached to a newly discovered and categorized denizen of the Willapa Hills, **Loomisiella pylei**, *a formerly undescribed millipede now doing honor to the esteemed local naturalist. As we wrap up our conversation, I ask Bob what — besides its admixture of salt and fresh water, and its relatively new history and settlement — personifies his beloved home, the Tidewater Reach.*

RMP: Well, in the first place, it's well documented that Oregonians and Washingtonians have had their differences over roots, and influences, and even self-image. So they may regard the river differently, too.

HRC: Is that just the accidents of history, of their migrations?

RMP: I heard a compelling lecture in which the speaker maintained that the group characteristics of Washingtonians and Oregonians were considerably different. He said that the Washingtonians primarily came by sea, and earlier. Whereas the Oregonians mostly arrived by overland trail, or by rail, later on, and were rather more conservative. That the Washingtonians, on the whole, were a more adventurous batch. I don't know if those qualities persist, but a case can be made that the Columbia is what binds them both. After all, they participated equally in removing the river, its banks, and the fish from the First Peoples, whose actual heritage it was until we arrived.

HRC: So, be adventurous. Let's hear a couple of generalizations as we wrap this up: Just what and who are we, we people of today's Tidewater Reach, and our neighbors? Do we have a unique world view, experience, character?

RMP: If I were going to generalize about people around the river — and this is pretty obvious — I would say one of them is a strong attraction to water, and to the edges of things.

HRC: Seems pretty safe to say.

RMP: Yes, but it's the notion of the edge, not just the water. The shore. I'm from Colorado and I still love the short grass prairie, and the mountains. But when I'm there I feel somehow constrained, as if I'm limited, because I can't get to a coast. The second thing I would name is an attraction for a moderate, maritime climate: the temperate rain forest and its inland shadow. And that can extend socially as well as physically. We don't have vast extremes of climate, which may also be a moderating factor on the culture. By no means are people here homogeneous, but they seem to promote and embrace, dare I say, a kind of civility or comity, a moderation toward one another and the land. At least I like to imagine such a thing!

HRC: I know Seattle and Portland both have that reputation as "mellow" that has to be due in part to their maritime climates. Perhaps?

RMP: And of course the fact that everyone here is from someplace else, so getting along with other people is pretty basic, since we're all migrants at some point. The third thing I would say, and this may be more personal, but I think it applies to a lot of other people, too, is an enigmatic sense of regional integrity combined with connection to the rest of the world. Perhaps that's the whole Pacific Rim thing. It means we are not that distant in time and evolution from the Polynesians and the Beringians. and therefore, from our more recent predecessors on the river.

HRC: Beringians? Help me?

RMP: The ancient Asians who came across the Beringian land bridge in what is now the Bering Sea, eons ago. They gave rise to many of the Native American cultures of today.

HRC: Certainly now we seem to be looking west, not east, more aligned to the Pacific cultures, trade partners, economics, than the old eastern-centric view we grew up with.

RMP: The old view was more Euro-centric. I think people here in The Reach feel a real kinship — in continuity with our native American precursors and our own, sometimes brutal discovery story — for this Pacific Ocean and these Pacific cultures.

HRC: What do you want people to take away from this latest piece of work, this pairing of words and pictures?

RMP: Both Judy and I have thought, though I guess we don't say it explicitly, of how much we love this river. We love its working parts, and we love how the people depend upon it, from the gillnetters to the writers and photographers, even the damned cruise ships. This is why we have both been deeply involved alongside many others in campaigns to protect the Columbia from inappropriate industry, as well as projects to conserve and restore fish and wildlife habitat. Everybody who comes here knows the river is essential. They care for the river — or they certainly should! The river makes us feel like caring. And to feel like caring is a better way to live than to be oblivious.

Portions of these interviews originated in the
Columbia River Reader, April 2018; April 2020
Interviews are edited for length and condensed for clarity,
Copyright MMXX
Columbia River Reader Press

Columbia River Reader Press